PRESENTED TO:

_____

FROM:

_____

DATE:

_____

Jesus calling®

FOR TEENS

50 DEVOTIONS FOR
BUSY DAYS

Sarah Young

Adapted by Tama Fortner

Edited by Kris Bearss

THOMAS NELSON
Since 1798

Published in Nashville, Tennessee, by Tommy Nelson. Tommy Nelson is an imprint of Thomas Nelson. Thomas Nelson is a registered trademark of HarperCollins Christian Publishing, Inc.

Unless otherwise noted, Scripture quotations used in this book are from: The Holy Bible, New International Version®. © 1973, 1978, 1984 by Biblica, Inc.™ Used by permission of Zondervan. All rights reserved worldwide. www.zondervan.com. The "NIV"and "New International Version" are trademarks registered in the United States Patent and Trademark Office by Biblica, Inc.™

Scripture quotations marked CEV are taken from the Contemporary English Version®, © 1995 American Bible Society. All rights reserved.

Scripture quotations marked ICB are taken from the International Children's Bible®. Copyright © 1986, 1988, 1999 by Thomas Nelson. Used by permission. All rights reserved.

Scripture quotations marked NASB are taken from the New American Standard Bible®, © 1960, 1962, 1963, 1968, 1971, 1972, 1973, 1975, 1977, 1995 by The Lockman Foundation. Used by permission.

Scripture quotations marked NKJV are taken from the New King James Version. © 1982 by Thomas Nelson. Used by permission. All rights reserved.

Scripture quotations marked NLT are taken the Holy Bible, New Living Translation © copyright 1996, 2004 by Tyndale House Foundation. Used by permission of Tyndale House Publishers, Inc., Carol Stream, Illinois 60188. All rights reserved.

ISBN 978-1-4003-2438-5

Library of Congress Cataloging-in-Publication Data

Fortner, Tama, 1969–
Jesus calling: 365 devotions for kids / Sarah Young; adapted by Tama Fortner; edited by Kris Bearss.
p. cm.
ISBN 978–1–4003–1634–2 (hardcover)
1. Devotional calendars—Juvenile literature. I. Young, Sarah, 1946–II. Bearss, Kris. III. Young, Sarah, 1946–Jesus calling. IV. Title.
BV4870.F67 2010
242'.62—dc22   2010017099

Printed in China

18 19 20 21 22 DSC 5 4 3 2 1

INTRODUCTION

We live among people who think staying busy is the best way to live. Even Christians often fall into the trap of thinking *more* is always better—more stuff, more work, sports, or activities. But this leads to a life that is on overload.

Jesus calls you to step away and spend time with Him. His Words fill your life with peace, joy, and rest.

The Bible is the only perfect Word of God—without errors. I always work hard to keep my writings consistent with the unchanging truths of Scripture.

I have written this devotional from the perspective of Jesus speaking, to help readers feel more personally connected with Him. So the first person singular ("I," "Me," "My," "Mine") always refers to Jesus; "you" refers to you, the reader. I've included Scripture references after each reading. Words from the Bible (some paraphrased, some quoted) are written in italics.

The devotions in this book are meant to be read slowly, preferably in a quiet place—with your Bible open. Spending time with Jesus will prepare you to get through this busy day successfully.

Sarah Young

NO SHORTCUTS

I have planned out a perfect path for your life, and I am leading you along that path. In the distance, you can see the mountaintop. That's our goal. I know that you want to go straight to the top, but don't take shortcuts. Follow Me instead. Shortcuts can take you into dangerous places.

There will be difficulties along the way, for sure. But I will use them to bless you with courage and strength. At times it might even seem that I am leading you away from the goal. Follow Me anyway. I have lovingly planned every inch of your journey.

Hold My hand and walk with Me. When the path gets rocky and steep—when problems get in your way—hold even tighter to My hand. Together we will make it to the top!

JOHN 21:19; 2 CORINTHIANS 4:17

The Lord God

gives me my

STRENGTH.

He makes me

like a deer, which

does not stumble.

He **LEADS** me safely

on the steep mountains.

—Habakkuk 3:19 (icb)

THE PIT OF SELF-PITY

It's easy to feel sorry for yourself—especially when things aren't going your way, or you feel like everyone is against you, or you are just plain tired of trying so hard all the time. But feeling sorry for yourself is one of the devil's favorite traps. Don't even go near it! Once you fall into his trap, it is very hard to get out again.

How can you protect yourself from the devil's traps? Focus on Me. When you are feeling sorry for yourself, you are thinking only about yourself and your problems. But when you think about Me and praise Me for My Presence, then you won't stumble into the pit of self-pity. Stay close to Me in your words and thoughts. I will give you the energy to run the race—and never give up!

PSALM 89:15–16; HEBREWS 12:2

So let us RUN

the race that

is before us and

NEVER give up.

—Hebrews 12:1 (ICB)

I LOVE YOU

I *love you*. Take a moment, be still, and think about that. I am the Creator of the universe, the Ruler of Time, the Master of all that you see—and I love *you*. My Love is so big that it fills up all of space, time, and eternity.

I know that you don't fully understand the hugeness of My Love for you. You see glimpses of it now—as you feel Me guiding you, drawing you closer to Me, and answering your prayers. But one day you will see Me face-to-Face. Then you will know exactly how wide and long and high and deep My Love for you really is. For now, just know that My Love is so huge it cannot be measured. And it goes with you through every moment of every day.

EPHESIANS 3:16–19

Now all we can

SEE of God is like a

cloudy picture in a mirror.

Later we will see him

face to face. We don't

KNOW everything, but

then we will, just as God

completely understands us.

—1 Corinthians 13:12 (CEV)

DON'T GO IT ALONE

It is a simple fact: You cannot make it by yourself. More importantly, you don't *have* to make it by yourself. It's up to you.

Yes, there will be days when everything goes just the way you planned. You've got everything under control, and you are living on top of the world. But then—BAM! Trouble—*big* trouble—comes and yanks away the control you thought you had. An illness, an accident, it's something you never saw coming.

You know you need help. Let Me help you. I already know the answers. Let Me guide you to them. But first you have to choose: Do you stubbornly go it alone? Or do you humbly come to Me and let Me help you? Please, choose Me.

JAMES 1:2–3

You are my help.

Because of your

PROTECTION,

I sing. I stay close

to you. You SUPPORT

me with your right hand.

—Psalm 63:7–8 (icb)

LIVE THIS DAY

Will you do well on your exam? Will your friend still be angry? Will you live up to what your parents expect from you? I know these kinds of things worry you. But your greatest danger is worrying about tomorrow.

Just as physically you can only carry so many heavy boxes, spiritually you can only carry so many burdens. *Today* is the only day you have to live. If you try to carry tomorrow's worries while you are living today, you will stumble and fall because the load is just too heavy. You must choose to live *this* day. Give your worries about tomorrow to Me, and I will carry them for you. I will be right beside you, holding your hand.

1 Corinthians 10:13

Yet I am **ALWAYS**

with you; you

HOLD me by my

right hand.

—Psalm 73:23

May the God of hope fill you with all joy and peace as you trust in him, so that you may overflow with hope by the power of the Holy Spirit.

—Romans 15:13

I AM ALWAYS

I am the Creator and Ruler of time and space. I am not subject to the same limitations that you are. I am able to be everywhere at every time.

I have always been with you. I know every struggle and every success that you have ever had. I am right here with you now, helping you through this day. And I go on ahead of you into the future, so that I know what is coming in your life and I can prepare you for it. I am *always*. I can be in yesterday, today, and tomorrow—and still never let go of your hand.

PSALM 37:3–4

So he is ALWAYS able to

save those who come to

God through him. He can

do this, because he always

LIVES, ready to help those

who come before God.

—HEBREWS 7:25 (ICB)

DEFEATING EVIL

If you learn to trust Me—*really* trust Me—with all your heart and soul, then nothing can separate you from My Peace. I can use all your problems—even huge ones—to train you in trusting Me. This is how you defeat the evil one. You let Me use the problems he throws your way to make you stronger.

Remember Joseph? His jealous brothers sold him into slavery in Egypt. But he never stopped trusting Me. So I was able to use that terrible thing to save not only Joseph and his family, but a whole nation of people.

Don't be afraid of what this day—or any day—might bring. Put your energy into trusting Me. Remind yourself that I am in complete control, and I can bring good out of any situation.

PSALM 23:4

You INTENDED to harm me, but God intended it all for GOOD. He brought me to this position so I could SAVE the lives of many people.

—GENESIS 50:20 (NLT)

NOTHING SURPRISES ME

I go before you as well as with you into this day. Nothing surprises Me. I know exactly what will happen—both the good and the bad. Trust in Me and don't be afraid. Stay close to Me, and I will not let you be overwhelmed by anything that happens today. I will help you through it all—fights with a friend, disappointments, a bad grade, temptations to sin, illness—whatever comes your way.

Don't go through today with fear in your heart because of what might or might not happen. I will help you deal with *whatever* happens—moment by moment. Facing your problems with Me brings blessings that are much bigger than your troubles. So bring all your problems to Me, and I will bless you with My Joy.

2 Corinthians 4:16–17

Yea, though I **WALK**

through the valley

of the **SHADOW** of death,

I will fear no evil;

for You are with me.

—Psalm 23:4 (NKJV)

I WILL NEVER LEAVE YOU

Nothing can separate you from My Love. *Nothing.* Not bullies, not tough times, not even Satan himself. I will never leave you.

Most of the misery in this world comes from feeling lonely and unloved. Especially when times are tough, people often feel that I have left them all alone. And that feeling can be even worse than the problems they are facing. But know this: I never leave you—not even for a second. I am constantly watching over you. If you feel alone or frightened, ask Me to comfort you with My Presence. Then repeat these promises to yourself: "Nothing can separate me from Your Love, Jesus. . . . You will never leave me."

ROMANS 8:38–39; ISAIAH 49:15–16

"No one will be able to **STAND** up against you all the days of your life. As I was with Moses, so I will be with you; I will **NEVER** leave you nor forsake you."

—Joshua 1:5

THE POSITION
OF YOUR HEART

I am the God of all time and of all that is. And I am waiting to hear from you—morning, noon, and night.

Don't just pray to Me in the quiet of the morning. Don't just pray to Me at church or when things are going well. And don't just pray to Me with your head bowed and your eyes closed. Talk to Me every day, at any time, in any place and situation—in class, on the soccer field, while practicing piano or doing homework or texting your friends. Pray when you're in trouble and when you're happy. Time with Me is what matters, not what time it is.

You can talk to Me lying down, sitting up, or with arms stretched up to heaven. Your eyes can be opened or closed. I don't care about the position of your body—I care about the position of your heart. And when your heart is seeking Me, I will hear you.

PSALM 32:6; PSALM 62:8

Morning, noon,

and night I CRY

out in my distress,

and the LORD

HEARS my voice.

—PSALM 55:17 (NLT)

So we fix our eyes not on what is seen, but on what is unseen. For what is seen is temporary, but what is unseen is eternal.

—2 Corinthians 4:18

SEARCH FOR ME

I want you to search for Me—not just once in a while, not just on Sundays, and not just when you need My help. I want you to look for Me at all times.

And I want you to search with all your heart and soul—not just because you think you should, or because someone told you to. Look for Me with everything that is in you because you want to find Me.

When you search for Me with all your heart and all your soul, you *will* find Me—and you will enjoy Love, Joy, and Peace in My Presence. I promise.

Seek Me in good times; seek Me in hard times. And you will find Me watching over you all the time.

HEBREWS 10:23; PSALM 145:20

From there you

will SEEK the Lord

your God, and you will

FIND Him if you search

for Him with all your

HEART and all your soul.

—Deuteronomy 4:29 (nasb)

NO OTHER
FRIEND LIKE ME

I am your best Friend, *and* I am your King.

My friendship is practical and down-to-earth. As your Friend, I am always here to listen and to help. Together we will face whatever each day brings: pleasures, hardships, adventures, disappointments.

But as your heavenly King, our friendship opens up so many more possibilities. As King, I can create something wonderful out of the ashes of lost dreams, Joy out of sorrow, and Peace out of problems.

And it's all because I love you. My Love for you is so great that I gave up heaven to come to earth as a helpless baby. It is so great that I lived in the dust and sin of this world. And it is so great that I died on the cross to save your soul. There is no other friend like Me!

JOHN 15:14–15; ISAIAH 61:3;
2 CORINTHIANS 6:10

"There is no

GREATER love

than to lay

down one's **LIFE**

for one's friends."

—John 15:13 (NLT)

COUNT IT AS GARBAGE

When your plans are messed up, talk to Me about it. Talking with Me blesses you and strengthens our friendship. Also, I take the sting out of your disappointment by making something good come of it. So you can be joyful, even when things are going wrong. But it takes practice.

Start by bringing Me small things—the bad grade, the rained-out game. Even small disappointments can focus your thoughts on yourself instead of Me. But when you talk with Me, you see that the things you've lost are nothing compared to the wonders of knowing Me.

You'll need a lot of practice before you can trust Me with big disappointments. But if you keep at it, someday even the greatest things of this world will seem like garbage compared to the Joy of knowing Me—your Savior, Lord, and Friend.

COLOSSIANS 4:2; PHILIPPIANS 3:7

Nothing is as wonderful

as **KNOWING** Christ Jesus

my Lord. I have given up

EVERYTHING else and

count it all as garbage.

All I want is Christ.

—PHILIPPIANS 3:8 (CEV)

YOUR HOPE AND
MY PROMISE

There is nothing that the evil one hates more than your closeness to Me. He will do anything to pull you away. So don't be surprised by his fiery attacks on your mind.

There is a massive spiritual war being fought every day. When you find yourself in the thick of the battle, cry out, "Jesus, help me!" At that very instant, the battle becomes Mine. Your job is simply to trust Me as I fight for you.

When My Name is used in the right way, it has unlimited Power to bless and protect. At the end of time, every knee will bow *at the Name of Jesus.* People who have used My Name as a swear word will tremble in fear. But all those who have used My Name to draw near Me will be filled with glorious Joy. This is your hope—and My promise to you.

1 SAMUEL 17:47; PHILIPPIANS 2:9-10;
1 PETER 1:8-9

For our **STRUGGLE** is not against flesh and blood, but against the rulers, against the authorities, against the powers of this dark world and against the **SPIRITUAL FORCES OF EVIL** in the heavenly realms.

—Ephesians 6:12

SAFE AND SECURE

You want to feel safe and secure. You say you trust Me, but in your private thoughts, you are still trying to fix your world so that it is safe and predictable. Not only is this an impossible goal, but it actually makes you *less* safe and secure.

True safety and security are found only in Me—in depending on My Presence. When your world seems unsteady and scary, grab My hand. I will hold tightly to you and keep you safe.

Instead of searching for a problem-free life, be glad that you have troubles. In the darkness of your trouble, you can see the brightness of My Face more clearly. This helps you feel closer to me.

So hold tightly to My hand, confident that today's problems have a purpose. And remember—you have an eternity of trouble-free living just waiting for you in heaven.

ISAIAH 41:10; JAMES 1:2

Even there

your hand will

GUIDE me,

your right hand

will HOLD me fast.

—Psalm 139:10

Jesus Christ never changes!
He is the same yesterday,
today, and forever.

—Hebrews 13:8 (CEV)

GRAB HOLD OF HOPE!

The hope of heaven. Too many of My children don't really understand what this means. When I talk of *hope*, it isn't just wishful thinking. This hope is My promise for all My children.

As soon as I became your Savior, heaven became your final, permanent home. But there are blessings of this hope that you can enjoy right now! Because your true home is heaven, you know that any troubles you face today are only temporary. *The hope of heaven* helps you through your tough times, brightening even the darkest days. It also helps you keep trusting that I am taking care of you—and everything will be all right.

Don't just wish for heaven—grab hold of the hope of heaven! Let its blessing fill your life today.

ROMANS 8:23–25; HEBREWS 6:19–20;

ROMANS 15:13

So God has given both his

PROMISE and his oath. These

two things are unchangeable

because it is IMPOSSIBLE

for God to lie. Therefore,

we who have fled to him

for refuge can have great

CONFIDENCE as we hold to

the hope that lies before us.

—Hebrews 6:18 (nlt)

TINY STEPS OF TRUST

Trust Me with every fiber of your being! The more you choose to trust Me, the more I can do in you and through you.

I want you to trust Me in the big things, the crisis moments, the important decisions. I also want you to trust Me in the small things, the everyday moments, the decisions you hardly even think about.

Trusting Me in the everyday things tells Me that your trust is a daily habit—*not* something you forget about until times get tough.

I care just as much about your tiny steps of trust as I do about your gigantic leaps of faith. You may think that no one notices, but the One who is always beside you sees everything—and rejoices!

PSALM 40:4; PSALM 56:3–4;
PSALM 62:8; ISAIAH 26:3

TRUST in the

LORD forever,

for the LORD,

the LORD, is the

Rock ETERNAL.

—ISAIAH 26:4

I AM BIGGER
THAN THE WORLD

Think about how wonderful it feels to dive into a cool pool of water on a hot summer's day. That is what My Peace is like. It will refresh you and strengthen you. And that peace can be yours at all times.

As you go through your day, you will face problems and troubles. But you *never* have to face them alone. I am *always* with you. I am the best Friend that you will ever have. I walk beside you, to give you comfort and strength. I also walk ahead of you, so that I am ready to help you face whatever is coming. And I am within you, giving you a secret ability to think and act without fear.

There will be problems and hard times, but don't let them get you down. I have already overcome all the problems of this world. In Me you can find Peace.

PSALM 31:19–20

"I have **TOLD** you

these things,

so that in me

you may have

PEACE. In this world

you will have trouble.

But take heart! I have

OVERCOME the world."

—John 16:33

DARE TO
DREAM MY DREAM

Dream your biggest, most incredible dream—and then know that I am able to do far more than that, far more than you could ever ask or imagine. Allow Me to fill your mind with *My* dreams for you.

Don't be discouraged if your prayers are not answered right away. Time is a great teacher. It teaches you to be patient and to trust in My perfect plan—even when you don't know what is going to happen next.

When everything seems way too hard, that is when you can truly see My Power at work in your life. Don't let this world's craziness drag you into worry. Instead, choose to see all that I am doing around you. Remember, there is no limit to what I can do.

ROMANS 8:6; ISAIAH 40:30–31;
REVELATION 5:13

Now to him who is able to do immeasurably more than all we ask or IMAGINE, according to his power that is at work within us, to him be GLORY in the church and in Christ Jesus throughout all generations, for ever and ever! Amen.

—Ephesians 3:20–21

A TREASURE OF TRUST

Every time you choose to trust Me, it's like putting a coin into My treasury. Like a bank, I keep these coins of trust safe for you. Over time, these coins add up, creating a wealth of trust for you to use when you need it. The more you choose to trust Me and My teaching, instead of just following your friends, the more I will help you trust Me.

Trusting takes practice. Start on quiet days, when nothing much seems to be happening. You will see that I really am faithful. Then, when trouble comes, you will know how to trust Me—because you have practiced. You will have saved up a heavenly treasure of trust that will see you through whatever troubles come your way.

PSALM 56:3—4

"But store up for yourselves treasures in HEAVEN, where moth and rust do not destroy, and where thieves do not break in and steal. For where your TREASURE is, there your heart will be also."

—Matthew 6:20-21

He makes me like a deer, which does not stumble. He helps me stand on the steep mountains.

—Psalm 1:33 (ICB)

NO NEED TO PRETEND

Everyone wants to look good. You want to wear the right clothes, fix your hair just so, and say just the right things. It's easy to clean up your outside, and make your friends think you have it all together on the inside. You can fool a lot of people that way. But not Me. I see straight through you. I understand who you really are, and *I love you*.

Talk to Me about your struggles, about the times when you feel that you just aren't good enough. Little by little, I will take those struggles and turn them into strengths. You don't have to pretend or put on a show with Me. Just be yourself. There is nothing you can do—or not do—that will stop Me from loving you.

ROMANS 8:38–39

"People LOOK at the outside of a person, but the Lord looks at the HEART."

—1 Samuel 16:7 (ICB)

DON'T REHEARSE
YOUR PROBLEMS

Some days are just hard—a tough test, a fight with a friend, trouble at home. You rehearse it over and over in your mind like the words to a song. But when you rehearse your problems that way, you live them over and over again. You were meant to live through them only once—when they actually happen!

Don't try to figure out how you'll get through this situation on your own. Come to Me, and let Me guide you and give you My Peace. Don't forget that I am always with you. I will give you all the strength and courage you need to face whatever challenges come your way. I will turn your worries and your fears into confidence and trust.

MATTHEW 11:28–30; JOSHUA 1:5

Be **STRONG** and

courageous. Do not

be terrified; do not

be discouraged, for the

Lᴏʀᴅ your God will be

with you **WHEREVER**

you go.

—Jᴏsʜᴜᴀ 1:9

I AM STILL HERE

When you seek Me, You will find more than you ever dreamed possible. I will replace your worries with peace, and I will shower you with blessings.

I am all that you are searching and hoping for. That empty place inside you? The one you've tried to fill with stuff, and friends, and so many other things? I am the only One who can fill it. Seek Me!

All the stuff and busyness of this world may sometimes distract you and take your attention away from Me. But I am watching and waiting for you to return to Me. And when you do search for Me again, you will find that I am still here with you—right where I have always been.

PHILIPPIANS 4:7; JEREMIAH 29:13

When You said,

"SEEK My face,"

My heart said to You,

"Your FACE, LORD,

I will seek."

—PSALM 27:8 (NKJV)

SHINE!

It's okay to be human. If your mind wanders while you are praying, don't be surprised or upset. Simply turn your thoughts back to Me, and know that I understand.

Don't let your prayer time be the only time you think about Me. Take time for Me throughout your day. Just whisper My Name. Say a simple prayer of thanks. Smile as you think about how much I love you. That is worship. Making these moments of worship a part of your day will create in you a gentle and quiet spirit. And that makes Me very happy.

As you grow closer to Me, the light of My Love will shine through you. Those around you will see it and be blessed.

DEUTERONOMY 31:6; 1 PETER 3:4;
2 CORINTHIANS 4:6–7; 2 CORINTHIANS 12:9

God once said, "Let the light SHINE out of the darkness!" And this is the same God who made his light shine in our HEARTS. He gave us light by letting us know the glory of God that is in the FACE of Christ.

—2 Corinthians 4:6 (ICB)

THE GREATEST
OF TREASURES

My Peace is the greatest of treasures. It is the most expensive of gifts, both for Me the Giver and for you the receiver. I bought this peace for you with My own blood. And to receive it, you must learn to trust Me in the middle of life's storms.

When everything is going your way, you have the peace of this world, and it is easy to forget about Me. But that kind of peace does not last. It cannot handle problems. It can't heal broken hearts, lost friendships, or big disappointments. But My Peace can. It can even find a way to turn troubles into blessings, making you stronger in your faith.

Expect troubles every day. They are just a part of living in an imperfect world. But when they come your way, be glad, for I have overcome this world— and all its troubles.

MATTHEW 13:46; JOHN 16:33

Dear brothers
and sisters,

when TROUBLES

come your way,

consider it an

OPPORTUNITY

for great joy.

—James 1:2 (nlt)

Now the Lord is the Spirit,
and where the Spirit of the
Lord is, there is freedom.

—2 Corinthians 3:17

CAPTURE
EVERY THOUGHT

I have given you an amazing gift—the freedom to choose. You may choose to think about anything you wish. I am asking that you choose to think about Me.

Today, let your goal be to capture every thought and bring it to Me. Wherever your mind wanders, lasso those thoughts and show them to Me. Having anxious thoughts? They shrivel up and disappear when My Light shines on them. Having confused thoughts? My Peace will untangle them. Starting to think you're better than someone else? My unconditional Love will help you see that I love all My children, and so should you. Keep your thoughts focused on Me so that you can enjoy My Peace.

PSALM 8:5; GENESIS 1:26–27; ISAIAH 26:3

We **CAPTURE**

every thought

and make it

give up and

OBEY Christ.

—2 Corinthians 10:5 (icb)

REST

When you're so tired you can hardly stand, doesn't it feel wonderful when you finally get to sink into your own bed? Your body relaxes; your breathing slows; your bones just seem to melt into the mattress. And you rest.

Just as your body gets tired, so does your spirit. Trying to do the right thing can really wear you out sometimes, especially if everyone around you is doing what's wrong. Sometimes you just need a break.

Come to Me. Lift up your hands in prayer to Me. Lie back and rest in My Presence. Take a deep breath of My Peace. I will refresh you and give you the strength to keep going.

MATTHEW 11:29; 1 TIMOTHY 2:8

Then Jesus said,

"**COME** to me, all of

you who are weary

and carry heavy

BURDENS, and I will

give you rest."

—MATTHEW 11:28 (NLT)

I WILL LIFT YOU UP

I am above all things: your problems, your disappointments and hurts, and all the ever-changing events that fill up this world. And I want to lift you above all these things too.

It's a fact: You will have problems in this life. You will stumble and fall into the dirt and dust of this world. But don't give up! Don't let the dirt and dust be the only thing you see. See Me! Reach out your hand and call out, "Help me, Jesus!"

I am always near you. I will grab your hand, and I will pull you up. I will dust you off and sit you beside Me. And I will show you how—together—we can get through it all.

MATTHEW 14:28–32

And God RAISED

us up with Christ

and SEATED us with

him in the heavenly

realms in Christ Jesus.

—Ephesians 2:6

I GIVE YOU PEACE

I give you Peace! These are the words I have been saying to My followers ever since I rose from the grave. I died like a criminal on the cross, but I did it for you. With My blood, I was able to purchase Peace for you. I wore a crown of thorns so that I could give you a crown of Peace.

How do you get My Peace? It is so simple. Find a quiet place, sit for a moment, think about Me, and thank Me for loving you so much. When you do this, I will come and sit beside you. I will wrap you up in My Peace like a warm blanket. This will keep your heart close to Mine.

JOHN 20:19; JOHN 14:27

Jesus

said,

"PEACE be

with you!"

—John 20:21

I WILL NEVER DISAPPOINT YOU

You live in a world that is constantly changing. Nothing—and no one—ever stays the same. The weather changes, you grow taller, your friendships change, your relationship with your parents changes, people move away, interests change . . . and on and on.

Not only does this world change, but it is a world filled with sin. The people around you are going to make mistakes. Your feelings will get hurt. You are going to mess up. If you count on this world—or the people in it—to make you happy and give you peace, sooner or later you will be disappointed.

True, never-ending Peace can come only from Me. Ask Me to fill your heart with My Love and Peace. I will never disappoint you.

Colossians 1:27

Let the

PEACE

of Christ rule

in your **HEARTS.**

—Colossians 3:15

the LORD replied, "My Presence will go with you, and I will give you rest."

—Exodus 33:14

I'M RIGHT BY YOUR SIDE

If something in your life is making you anxious, come talk to Me about it. I am your best Friend—the one who always wants to hear from you, no matter what time of day or night it is.

When you pray, tell me what you need and then thank Me. Thank Me for listening. Thank Me for answering. And thank Me for the chance to trust Me more. You see, I use your tough times to make you a better, stronger person.

The world has it backward. The world says if you have enough money, enough stuff, the right friends, then you will have peace and security. But money and stuff can be stolen, and friends can let you down. True peace and security come only from Me. All you have to do is ask—I'm always right by your side.

PHILIPPIANS 4:6

You, Lord, give

TRUE peace. You

give peace to those

who **DEPEND** on you.

You give peace to

those who trust you.

—Isaiah 26:3 (icb)

WORRY WORMS

Have you ever seen a worm try to wriggle back into the dirt? That is what worry is like. It is constantly trying to wriggle its way back into your mind.

In this life, there will always be something that you *could* worry about. Something that just isn't quite right. That is part of living in an imperfect world. But worry can't do anything except tie you up into knots.

So how do you get rid of those worry worms? Keep your thoughts on Me. Think about how much I love you, how you can serve Me, and how I bless and protect you. When your mind is all filled up with Me, there's no room for worry worms.

1 Thessalonians 5:16–18

"Who of you by

worrying can ADD

a single hour to his life?

Since you cannot do this

very LITTLE thing, why do

you worry about the rest?"

—Luke 12:25–26

A JOY NO ONE CAN STEAL

You will have troubles. There will be sadness and hardship and hurt. But do not let these things take over your life. Don't let them be all that you think about. Learn to live above your troubles.

How is that possible? Through Me. When you spend a few minutes every day just sitting quietly with Me, I can give you the power to face your problems with a smile. You will begin to see your struggles as I see them. I will help you decide what is important and what is not. And I will fill your mind with Peace and Joy that no one can take away from you. I have already overcome the troubles of this world, and I will help you do the same with your problems.

John 16:33

"Now you are sad.

But I will see you

AGAIN and you will

be happy. And no one

will take **AWAY** your joy."

—John 16:22 (icb)

LIGHTEN UP!

Lighten up! Share a laugh with Me!

You thought you would never hear Me say that, but I love to laugh. After all, I created laughter! Look at some of the animals I made—monkeys, giraffes, zebras, and camels. Can you see now that I like to laugh, to be creative, to have fun?

Don't take yourself so seriously. It's okay to make a mistake. Everyone stumbles and falls. Everyone does something embarrassing sometimes. Learn to laugh at yourself, and don't worry if other people laugh along. Besides, You have Me on your side, so what are you worried about?

Go ahead, share a joke with Me. Clown around a bit—and we'll have a laugh together.

PHILIPPIANS 4:13

A happy

HEART is like

good medicine.

But a broken

spirit drains your

STRENGTH.

—Proverbs 17:22 (ICB)

I SPEAK TO YOU IN LOVE

†his world is full of voices. Often they are harsh and hurtful. They say, "You should have done better"; "You really messed up this time"; and "You just don't have what it takes." They can crush you and make you feel worthless.

These voices are not from Me. Even when you make a mistake, I don't reject you or shame you. I speak words of love and forgiveness. I lift you up and tell you the truth. And the truth is that you *do* have what it takes, because I live in you.

Listen to My voice and then let Me speak through you. When you find yourself in a tough situation, pause for a minute and let Me give you the words to say. Hasty words leave no room for Me. Let Me use your words to lift up those around you.

ROMANS 8:2; COLOSSIANS 1:27;
1 CORINTHIANS 6:19

Therefore, there

is now no

CONDEMNATION

for those who are

in Christ Jesus.

—ROMANS 8:1

Be joyful because you have hope.
Be patient when trouble comes.
Pray at all times.

—Romans 12:12 (icb)

LIKE A LITTLE CHILD

Sometimes you hear people say, "I wish you would grow up!" But I have a different message for you: "Keep trusting Me—*like a little child.*"

Small children trust Me so easily. They hear the song "Jesus Loves Me," and they believe every single word, without question. But as you grow up, the world tries to pull you away from trusting Me. It wants you to trust money, or stuff, or just doing whatever feels right to you. Don't give in to the world.

I have so much that I want to give you. I poured out My Life on the cross so that I could give you forgiveness and a home in heaven. And all I ask is that you trust Me—like a little child.

PHILIPPIANS 2:17; ISAIAH 26:3

"I tell you the truth.

You must ACCEPT

the kingdom of God

as a little child accepts

things, or you

will never ENTER it."

—Mark 10:15 (ICB)

EVERYTHING IN
ITS OWN TIME

Stop trying to work things out before their time has come. You can't take Friday's math test on Thursday. You can't celebrate your August birthday in June. And you can't make My will happen before the right time.

Accept that you must live one day at a time. When something pops into your mind, take a moment to ask Me whether it's part of My plan for you today—or not. If it isn't, trust Me to take care of it. Then forget about it, and concentrate on what you need to do *today*.

Your life will be much less complicated and confusing. There is a time for everything—and I will help you do everything I want you to do, in its own time.

JOHN 16:33

There is a **TIME**

for everything,

and a season for

every **ACTIVITY**

under heaven.

—ECCLESIASTES 3:1

GETTING RID
OF THE WEEDS

I promise to meet all your needs. And while you may not realize it, your greatest need is for My Peace.

I am the Gardener of your heart, planting seeds of peace. But the world also tosses in seeds. These seeds grow into weeds of pride, worry, and selfishness. If these weeds aren't ripped out quickly, they will choke out all your peace.

I get rid of those weeds in different ways. Sometimes, when you sit quietly in prayer, My Light shines on the weeds and they shrivel up. But other times, I use troubles to encourage you to trust Me. And that trust kills the weeds.

So thank Me for troubles, as well as joys. Because I use them both to make your heart My garden of Peace.

PHILIPPIANS 4:19

These little TROUBLES

are getting us ready for

an eternal GLORY that

will make all our troubles

SEEM like nothing.

—2 Corinthians 4:17 (cev)

I AM WAITING

I created your body to live in this world—to breathe, to run, and to rest. But I also designed you to be filled with the things of heaven—My Love, My Joy, and My Peace.

No matter how many mistakes you make, I am always waiting to fill you with My Spirit. In fact, when you are full of sadness for something you have done, that is when My Light can shine brightest in your life.

Spend some time alone with Me each day. Give Me all your cares, worries, and sadness. My Spirit will fill you with strength and confidence as you trust Me and walk in My ways.

2 CORINTHIANS 4:7

"In repentance and rest is your **SALVATION**, in quietness and trust is your **STRENGTH**."

—Isaiah 30:15

MY TRAINING PROGRAM

You are in training, and I am your coach. I am training you to keep your thoughts on Me.

You live in a world filled with sights and sounds. Some are good, and some are bad. But I don't want even the good things to take your attention away from Me.

This kind of focus takes training—just like practicing for a sport or a spelling bee. Just as some days you're in a zone where you almost can't miss a shot or misspell a word, some days your thoughts are on Me. Other days, nothing goes right, and every little thing distracts you from Me.

Don't let this throw you. When something grabs your attention, that's okay. Talk to Me about it. If it's a good thing, we'll rejoice together. If it's a problem, we'll work it out together. The key is *together*. When you're together with Me, you will have My Peace.

PSALM 112:7

"I will make you

STRONG and

will help you.

I will **SUPPORT**

you with my right

hand that **SAVES** you."

—Isaiah 41:10 (icb)

Now may the Lord of peace himself give you peace at all times and in every way. The Lord be with all of you.

—2 Thessalonians 3:16

PEACE FOR TODAY

When Moses and the Israelites were wandering in the desert, they were given manna to eat. Each morning they gathered just enough for that day. They could not store it for the future. This day-by-day gathering helped them remember that they needed Me—every day.

My Peace works in much the same way. When you come to Me in prayer with a thankful heart, I give you enough Peace for today. I will not give you enough for tomorrow—only today. That is because I want you to come to Me again tomorrow—and each day after that.

If I gave you enough Peace to last your whole life, you might fall into the trap of thinking you didn't need Me. I designed you to need Me every minute. So come to Me every day with a thankful attitude, knowing that I will give you Peace for today.

EXODUS 16:14–20; PHILIPPIANS 4:6–7, 19

Let us then

APPROACH the throne

of grace with confidence,

so that we may RECEIVE

mercy and find grace to

help us in our time of need.

—Hebrews 4:16

I WON'T
LEAVE YOU—EVER

Do not be afraid, for I am with you—always! No matter what happens, I will never abandon you. Think about that. Let that soak into your mind and heart.

If you get angry and say something that you shouldn't—I'm still with you.

If you take the easy way out and tell a lie to cover up something you did wrong—I'm still with you.

If you forget about Me and try to live life the way you want to—I'm still with you.

Sometimes the things you do will make Me happy. Sometimes the things you do will make Me sad. But there is nothing you can do that will **ever** make Me leave you.

MARK 4:39; PSALM 46:2; PSALM 73:23–24

Be strong and courageous.

Do not be AFRAID or terrified

because of them, for the

LORD your God goes with

you; he will NEVER leave

you nor forsake you.

—DEUTERONOMY 31:6

HERE-AND-NOW

I have lovingly created a path for your life. Nothing is by accident. Every twist, every turn, is a part of My plan.

Don't try to see what is up ahead on your path. And don't keep turning around and looking at the past. *Here-and-Now* is the only place you can live. When you are constantly looking at the past or the future, today slips through your fingers, half-lived. Don't worry about the test you blew last week. Don't worry about whether or not you'll get invited to that party next week. Letting go of past and future worries frees you up to enjoy the Here-and-Now.

Today is the day that is filled with My glorious Presence. Today is the day I have filled with blessings. Today is the day I give you My Peace.

LUKE 12:25–26

God will help those

who live in **DARKNESS**,

in the fear of death.

He will guide us into

the path that goes

TOWARD peace.

—Luke 1:79 (icb)

I AM LORD!

I am your Lord! I am the Friend who is always with you, but you must remember that I am also your Lord. I am King over all. And I want to be the King of your life.

As you begin each day, talk to Me about it. And as you go through your day, keep checking in with Me. Keep asking for My guidance. It's okay to make some plans, but be open to changes in those plans. I may have other ideas for your day.

Don't try to skip ahead or take shortcuts. Concentrate on the task that is right before you. Do your very best at that. Then trust Me to show you what to do next. I will guide you step by step, leading you along a path of peace.

LUKE 1:79

Many are the

PLANS in a

man's heart,

but it is the Lord's

PURPOSE that prevails.

—Proverbs 19:21

NEVER ALONE

There is a battle being fought for the control of your mind. The devil is using every weapon he can think of to win. He'll distract you—with fun, with busyness, and with noise. He'll plague you with fears, worries, and guilt over past mistakes. He'll do whatever it takes to keep your thoughts centered on yourself and away from Me.

But you are not alone in this battle. I am on your side, and I will fight with you. Your job is to call on My Spirit for help. Ask My Spirit to take control of your mind and keep your thoughts focused on Me. Then I will strengthen you so that you can withstand the devil's attacks. And I will fill your mind with Peace.

Isaiah 12:2

If a person's THINKING is controlled by his sinful self, then there is death. But if his thinking is controlled by the SPIRIT, then there is life and peace.

—Romans 8:6 (icb)

After the earthquake came a fire, but the Lord was not in the fire. And after the fire came a gentle whisper.

—1 kings 19:12

LIKE A CANDLE

At times you feel so weak and tired that you just don't know if you have the energy to keep going. You feel like the flame of a candle that is flickering and about to burn out.

Perhaps you think about coming to Me, but you are afraid I will demand something else of you. And you are just so tired. Or perhaps you worry that I will see your weakness as a lack of faith. So you avoid Me.

It's okay to be tired. It's okay to be weak. I understand how difficult things have been. I don't want to judge you. I just want to wrap you up in My everlasting arms and let you rest. Forget about the world, forget the things you need to do, forget the pressures—just come to Me and rest.

ISAIAH 54:10; ROMANS 8:26

He will not

crush the WEAKEST

reed or put out a

FLICKERING candle.

—Isaiah 42:3 (nlt)

FOCUSING YOUR THOUGHTS

Start your morning with Me. Resist that urge to roll over for just a few more minutes of sleep. Don't fill your room with music or television just yet. Take a few moments to center your thoughts on Me. And let Me fill you with My Joy and Peace.

Then as you go through your day, keep your thoughts focused on Me and My blessings. Pay attention to the things that are best—the things that are worth taking time for—like a true friend, the honor of a grandparent, the pure innocence of a baby, or the loveliness of My creation. Whatever is excellent and good, notice these things and praise Me for them. They are My blessings for you this day.

Isaiah 40:31; Psalm 27:4

Fix your thoughts on what

is true, and HONORABLE, and

right, and pure, and lovely,

and admirable. Think about

things that are EXCELLENT

and worthy of praise.

—Philippians 4:8 (NLT)

THE LIGHT OF THE SON

I came to this earth to give Light to the world. It's different from the sun's light, which makes the trees and plants grow. The Light of My Love shines brighter than any sun ever could.

The Light of My Presence that you see now is only a hint of what heaven will be like. I cannot show you all of My Light now; it would blind you. But in heaven you will be able to see the fullness of My Glory. My Light shines so brightly in heaven that there is no need for a sun, moon, or stars. My Light chases away all the darkness.

I can also chase away the darkness from your life. Just spend time with Me each day, letting My Light soak into your soul. This will help you look forward to seeing the Light of heaven—where you will see Me in all My Glory.

PSALM 4:6–8

The city does not need
the sun or the moon to
shine on it. The GLORY of
God is its light, and the
LAMB is the city's lamp.

—REVELATION 21:23 (ICB)

YOU ARE GOOD ENOUGH

You are good enough for Me to love. Just as you are. You don't have to do anything big or spectacular. You don't have to earn My Love or fight for My attention. All you have to do is lie back, close your eyes, and rest in My Love for you. I will wrap you up in the warm, soft blanket of My unconditional Love, which never ends. I don't want you to worry any more about being good enough to be loved.

Look into My eyes. There is no condemnation there. You have nothing to fear because you are My child—and I took the punishment for *all* your sins. So I'm not thinking about your mistakes or what you should have done or wishing you'd worked harder. When you look into My eyes, you will see only kindness, delight, and unending Love.

JOHN 15:13; ZEPHANIAH 3:17; NUMBERS 6:26

May the Lord

SHOW you his

kindness.

May he have

MERCY on you.

—Numbers 6:25 (icb)

THE TREASURE

I died a criminal's death to buy you the gift of Peace. But instead of accepting My gift, it sometimes seems that you're ignoring it. You hold on to your worries, fears, and loneliness so tightly that you can't receive My Peace. It hurts Me to see you all tied up in anxious knots. This is not what I want for you.

You feel you are too busy and stressed to bring your problems to Me. But here's the truth: The busier and more stressed you are, the more you need to spend time with Me. Take a deep breath, and then take another one—and another. Be still in My Presence. Let My Peace grow inside you as you trust Me with all your worries. Hold on to My gift of Peace like the treasure that it is.

PSALM 46:10; NUMBERS 6:25

The LORD **TURN**

his face

toward you

and give

you peace.

—NUMBERS 6:26

"But seek first his kingdom and
his righteousness, and all these
things will be given to you as well."
—Matthew 6:33